Humble Table, Wise Fare:
Hospitality for the Heart (II)

By Venerable Master Hsing Yun
Translated by Dr. Tom Manzo and Dr. Shujan Cheng

ISBN: 1-929192-01-0

Library of Congress Catalog
LC Control Number

99 075442

Translated from Chinese by Dr. Tom Manzo and Dr. Shujan Cheng
Cover by Shih Mei-Chi
Illustrated by Chu Sheng-Chun
Printed by Hsi Lai University Press
Printed in the United States of America
First edition, August, 1999.

Preface

<u>The Vegetable Root Sayings</u> is a Chinese book that was written by Hung Tz-Cheng during the Ming Dynasty. Since that time, numerous editions have been printed, with some copies being distributed for free. Some editions have contained graceful illustrations; a few years ago, the famous Taiwanese cartoonist Tsai Chih-Chung produced one such edition, complete with cartoons. I have also heard the book is currently widely distributed in Mainland China as well. These illustrated editions have increased the circulation of the book. The illustrations not only make the book more enjoyable to read, but also help people understand the principle of personal conduct. The merits from promoting the book's distribution are really boundless.

When I was young, I often read <u>The Vegetable Root Sayings</u>, familiarizing myself with the content of the book. Later, when I was preaching the Dharma, I was able to quote from the book. Over time, I have found that <u>The Vegetable Root Sayings</u> is not only brief, to the point, tactful and charming, but also rich in philosophical and literary gracefulness; it is popular and yet august. The literary and artistic meaning is so profound and lasting that each saying can serve as a motto for dealing with people and conducting affairs in daily life.

For more than thirty years, everything I have said and done has been for the purpose of preaching the Dharma and educating people's minds. Recently, it occurred to me that some of what I have said has the same style as <u>The Vegetable Root Sayings,</u> and that a collection of these could be dedicated to the youth of today to serve as a reference for cultivating body and mind. Joyfully aware of this possibility, some of my Fo Guang Shan disciples began to collect my lectures, diary entries, Dharma talks and opening speeches – more than 2,000 items in all. For the publication of <u>Roots of the Dharma</u> I have selected one thousand of these.

I have four hopes for this publication:

1) The content of this book is a selection of words that I have spoken to all levels of people. At this time our society is promoting spiritual reform. I sincerely hope that, by reading this book, people will feel the benefit of increasing merits and purifying the body and mind and consequently make some contribution to society.

2) I have been busy travelling throughout the world preaching the Dharma. There are always thousands of people who attend these events; however, I regret that I have no way of talking to every individual devotee and friend directly and leisurely. By dedicating this book to them, I hope that it can serve as a bridge to connect our hearts together, and thus, to some degree, reduce my regret.

3) In modern education there is a serious lack of books that encourage and promote learning and the cultivation of body and mind. I hope that this book can be used as a reference and guidebook to cultivating the mind for numerous students, and that it can profoundly influence their future.

4) <u>Roots of the Dharma</u>, like the old <u>The Vegetable Root Sayings</u>, is not like delicious gourmet food, but rather like the plain vegetables that go with the simple meal. I hope readers can be spiritually invigorated and completely relaxed and happy at this humble table.

Hsing Yun
Hsi Lai Temple
Los Angeles
August 1998

Acknowledgements

We wish to thank all those who had helped made this book possible. First and foremost, our greatest gratitude are extended to the husband and wife translating team, Dr. Tom Manzo and Dr. Shujan Cheng.

Dr. Manzo's credentials include a Ph.D. from Yale University, in literature. He received his Bodhisattva Precepts in 1997 on his first visit to Hsi Lai Temple. Currently, he is a faculty member at San Antonio College, Texas. Dr. Cheng holds a Ph.D. degree in Finance. Originally from Taiwan, she has been a resident in the U.S. for the past ten years. A Buddhist for many years, she received her Bodhisattva Precepts several years ago.

We also like to thank Venerable Miao-Chieh, Susan Tidwell, and Amy Lam for their dedicated efforts during our translation process. Our appreciations also go to everyone who has supported this project from its conception to completion.

Cultivate interests,
But don't become obsessed.
Learn to be morally upright,
But don't become ultraconservative.

培養興趣，而不養成癖好；學習正直，而不學成古板。

Only through action,
Can we accomplish a goal.
Only through contemplation and practice,
Can we reach nirvana.

唯有付諸行動，才能達到目標；唯有真修力行，才能航行波岸。

Searching for Truth
Is the highest human hope.
Propagating Truth
Is the ultimate human mission.

探索眞理是人類最大的希望，傳播眞理是人類最高的使命。

The program of education
Is to stimulate the mind.
The key to education
Is to instruct according to potential.
The foundation of education
Resides in the habits of daily life.
The purpose of education
Is to develop character.

教育的課程在啟發心智，教育的要訣在觀機逗教，教育的基礎在生活習慣，教育的目的在完成人格。

4

If the reasoning is unclear,
It's difficult to accomplish things.
If things don't transpire,
It's difficult to demonstrate the reasoning.

理不明，事難辨；事不舉，理難證。

Knowledge is knowing how to question
Even after you have learned.
Peregrination knowledge is to learn more
Even after you have journeyed it.

學問，學了要會問；參學，參了還要學。

Although carelessness
May easily result in mistakes,
Over-carefulness
Can easily spoil things as well.

粗心大意固然容易做錯事，太過細心執著也容易誤事。

Being mindful everywhere,
One observes problems.
Researching everything,
One resolves them.

處處留心，能夠發現問題；事事研究，能夠解決問題。

The best negotiation approach
Is to start with what is beneficial
To the other party.
The greatest affinity created
Is to help others
To succeed.

最好的談判，是從對方的利益著手；最大的結緣，是幫助別人獲致成功。

To outside temptation
You must be as unenticed
As still water and dead ashes.
To the pursuit of knowledge
You must be as vigorous
As a wildfire.

對外境之誘惑，必要如止水死灰；對學識之仰望，必要能如火如荼。

The way to longevity
Is through character, achievement and ideas.
The way to prosperity
Is through credibility, responsibility and diligence.

立德、立功、立言，乃長壽之道；信用、責任、勤勞，乃發財之道。

Give people confidence,
Give people joy,
Give people hope,
Give people convenience –
Giving has limitless,
ingenious uses.

給人信心、給人歡喜、給人希望、給人方便；給，有無限的妙用。

Understand tolerance,
Understand peace,
Understand modesty,
Understand respect –
Understanding provides limitless,
Ingenious solutions.

懂得包容、懂得和平、懂得謙讓、懂得尊重;懂,有無限的妙解。

Know how to listen –
You will accept the teachings.
Know how to think –
You will benefit from the teachings.
Know how to cultivate –
You will apply the teachings.

會「聞」，於道才能接受；會「思」，於道才能受用；會「修」，於道才能奉行。

The wise nourish the mind.
The foolish nourish the body.
The ethical nourish virtues.
The sly nourish power.

15 　智者養神，愚者養身，君子養德，小人養威。

No money, no opportunity –
Let it be,
Cultivate merit and wisdom to reach nirvana.
Little clothing, little food –
Let it be,
Seek treasure in your mind.

無錢無緣由他去，只修福慧作慈航；少衣少食不計較，只求心內有寶藏。

When stating opinions,
Don't be afraid of being coarse and shallow,
But rather
Being childish and meaningless.
When beginning to write,
Don't worry about having no material,
But rather
About having no words and substance.

發言不懼粗淺，只懼幼稚無義；下筆不愁無文，只愁辭窮無物。

Making good use of fragments of time
Is a good recipe for making progress.
Treasuring every bit of opportunity
Is the wonder drug for conducting worldly affairs.

善用瑣碎的時間，是進步的良方；珍惜點滴的因緣，是處世的妙藥。

Don't use up your authority
Or you will collapse.
Don't use up your fortune and merits
Or you will decay.

勢力不可使盡，勢盡則傾；福德不可享盡，福盡則衰。

Passion is momentary,
Genuine passion lasts a lifetime.
Joy is momentary,
Genuine joy lasts a lifetime.

感動是一時的，真正的感動是一生的。受用是一時的，真正的受用是一生的。

Without words,
With complete, heart-to-heart understanding,
Is the most artistic form of communication.
Without notions,
With everything in complete understanding,
Is the highest form of doing things.

無言、心心相應，是談話的最高藝術；無相、事事默契，是做事的最高境界。

Knowing how to read books
Is not as good as knowing
How to read people.
Knowing how to read people
Is not as good as knowing
How to understand people.

會讀書不如會讀人，會讀人不如會識人，

Knowing how to understand people
Is not as good as knowing
How to utilize people.
Knowing how to utilize people
Is not as good as knowing
How to get along with people.

會識人不如會用人，會用人不如會做人。

All phenomena are conditional;
Don't try to force events.
Only if causes and conditions exist,
Will everything be fulfilled.

萬法相互緣起，世事不必強求；只要因緣具足，自能水到渠成。

Experience
Can teach people cleverness;
Suffering losses
Can teach people caution.

經驗能教人聰明，吃虧能教人謹慎。

Where justice is, don't fall behind.
Where profit is, don't jump ahead.

義之所在，不落人後；利之所在，不居人前。

26

If your honesty is unfocused,
Then your mind cannot concentrate.
If your faith is unfocused,
Then your words cannot be carried out.

誠不一，則心不能專；信不一，則言不能行。

Experience joy through modesty.
Cultivate virtue through tolerance.
Overcome desire through self-control.
Calm body and mind through peace.

從謙虛中體驗樂趣，從忍辱中培養美德，從自制中克服物欲，從寧靜中安頓身心。

Gathering and educating the world's talent
Is a pleasure in life.
Being close to a master and learning from him
Is a blessing in life.

聚天下之英才而教育之，乃人生之樂事也；得親近一明師而學習之，乃人生之福報也。

Virtues –
Don't reject them for being old.
Knowledge –
Don't reject it for being new.

Dreams
Open the door to idealism.
Idealism
Paves the way to success.

夢想打開理想之門，理想開闢成功之路。

The joy from contentment
Is limitless.
The suffering from greed
Is endless.

滿足之樂樂無彊，多欲之苦苦難了。

Those who are suspicious are suspected.
Those who are neglectful are neglected.

疑於人者，人亦疑之；忘於物者，物亦忘之。

Dust is not really tiny;
The cosmos is not huge.
One is not really trivial;
A billion is not plenty.

微塵不算小，虛空不算大；一個不算少，萬億不算多。

Happiness is nothing more
Than being free from worry.
Suffering is nothing more
Than having excessive desires.
Wealth is nothing more
Than being content.
Poverty is nothing more
Than being greedy.

35

樂莫大於無憂，苦莫大於多欲，富莫大於知足，貧莫大於貪婪。

Those who constantly strengthen their virtues
By reforming their ways
Are called good people.
Those who worsen their vices
By covering their mistakes
Are called common people.

Those who treasure wisdom manage
Not only profit,
But also culture.
Those who pursue kindness manage
Not only self,
But also morality and justice.

樂智者，經營利益，更經營文化；求仁者，經營自我，更經營道義；

Those who cherish rituals manage
Not only wealth,
But also good company.
Those who admire the teachings manage
Not only happiness,
But also inner bliss.

好禮者，經營財富，更經營善友；慕道者，經營快樂，更經營法喜。

38

Learning, and being able to apply it,
Is real learning.
Knowing, and being able to implement it,
Is real knowing.
Real learning and real knowing
Is wisdom.

學而能用，是真學；知而能行，是真知；真學真知，是智慧。

In learning Ch'an, first learn to be modest,
Then the Ch'an mind exists.
In cultivating purity, first cultivate respect,
Then the pure land exists.

學「禪」，先要學慚愧，自知慚愧才有禪心；修「淨」，首須修恭敬，能恭敬人才有淨土。

Learning Buddhism is to learn
Mainly about yourself;
So you must search for, and inquire
Into the original mind.
Learning Ch'an is to apply
Your own mind;
So you must investigate and study
The real self.

學佛，主要是學自己，所以要向自己本心尋問；學禪，主要是參自心，所以要向本來面目探究。

Knowledge makes people humble.
Ignorance makes people arrogant.
Modesty makes people noble.
Conceit makes people shallow.

學問使人謙虛，無知使人驕傲；虛心使人高貴，自負使人膚淺。

Knowledge
Is acquired through experiences,
Talent
Is shown through events.

學問是從經驗中獲得，才華是從事實中表現。

When learning,
Emulate the saint and the sage.
When comparing,
Use the saint and the sage as standards.

學習，應向聖賢看齊；比較，當以聖賢為準。

With some exposure to Buddhism,
One will make earnest efforts to cultivate virtue
And achieve morality.
With some grasp of the universe,
One will make further progress
And improve more.

擁有一些佛緣，才會精進不懈，成就道業；擁有一些天地，才會百尺竿頭，更進一步；

With some cultivation,
One will live simply
And live comfortably.
With some virtue,
One will easily meet one's needs
And take what one needs.

擁有一些修行，才會隨喜自在，不受拘束；擁有一些功德，才會隨意所需，隨意所取。

Although being a leader is good
Because you can lead the community,
Being second is also wonderful
Because you can complement and support others.
A leader should take care of the weak;
Number two should respect the elder.

擔當「老大」，能夠領導群倫，固然很好；作個「老二」，配合成就他人，也很偉大。老大要能愛護弱小，老二要能尊重前輩。

Trees won't grow tall
Without enduring the sun and the rain.
Character won't form completely
Without being tempered
By hardship and suffering.

樹木不經日曬雨淋長不高，人格未經千錘百鍊不健全。

By comprehending "no-self",
You realize letting go of self,
Merging into all beings,
And having more.

懂得「無我」，能夠放下小我，融入大我，方能擁有更多；

By experiencing "no-self",
You can understand giving and forsaking,
Sharing with all beings,
And having self everywhere.

體悟「無我」，懂得布施喜捨，分享眾生，就能處處有我。

With the public,
Get along in harmony.
With money,
Make good use.
With clothing and food,
Be sparing.
With body and mind,
Purify them and make them august.
With nature,
Be one, in mutual respect.

我與大眾要融和共處，我與金錢要能知善用，我與衣食要惜福不奢，我與身心要淨化莊嚴，我與自然要同體共生

The sage, who knows eternity,
Knows how to utilize time.
The saint, who knows boundlessness,
Knows how to utilize space.

懂得利用時間的人，便是懂得永恆的智者；懂得利用空間的人，便是懂得無邊的聖者。

Medicine is not good or bad;
When it cures, it is good.
Dharma is not superior or inferior;
When it is suitable, it is superior.

藥無好歹，癒病者良；法無勝劣，相應者勝。

The purpose of study
Is to have understanding.
The purpose of education
Is to get along with people.

讀書的目的，在於明理；教育的目的，在於做人。

Reform comes from determination.
Innovation comes from concentration.
Education comes from compassion.
Service comes from willingness.

改革來自決心，創造來自用心，教育來自愛心，服務來自發心。

The right way to study is nothing more
Than to read more,
And to memorize more.
The path to writing is nothing more
Than to think more,
And to write more.

讀書的竅門無他，多讀、多記而已；寫作的門路無他，多思、多寫而已。

Study can improve one's self;
Teaching can improve one even more.
Paying respect to the Buddha
Can give one confidence;
Practicing Buddhism
Can give one even more confidence.

讀書能進步，教書更能進步；拜佛有信心，行佛更有信心。

To show rightness,
One must first destroy evil;
To spread the pure,
One must first eliminate the impure.

顯正首要破邪，揚清必先激濁。

By observing a tree's shadow,
You know its height.
By observing a person's intention,
You know the person's virtue.

觀樹之陰影而知其高大，觀人之存心而知其德行。

Purifying the mind
Is the fundamental goal of education.
Changing temperament
Is the greatest benefit of studying.

淨化人心，是教育的根本目標；變化氣質，是讀書的最大受用。

Have the real recognition
Of the concept of time and space.
Have historical knowledge
Of the concept of tradition.
Have the universal recognition
Of the concept of culture.
Have truthful recognition
Of the concept of belief.

要有時空觀念的真實認知，要有傳統觀念的歷史認知，要有文化觀念的普遍認知，要有信仰觀念的真理認知

Being diligent,
You naturally have more time than others.
Being willing to move,
You naturally have broader space than others.
Being able to endure hardships,
You naturally have more success than others.

勤勞，時間自然比他人多；肯動，空間自然比他人廣；耐苦，成功自然比他人大。

The idea of the Buddha
Exceeds divine power;
You are in charge of your own destiny.
The idea of the pure land
Can achieve the ideal of human rights;
Foster the state of equality.

佛陀的主張是超越神權的控制，掌握自我的命運；淨土的理念能達到生權的理想，建立平等的國度

If you can enjoy the Buddha's teachings,
You can resolve things.
If you observe the Buddha's teachings,
You can live at ease.

若能受用佛法，才能解決事情；若能依止佛法，才能自在生活。

Observe the precepts,
Or you will cut off
The road to the human and heaven realms.
Cultivate virtue,
Or meritorious work will be incomplete.
Study sutras,
Or logical thought will be unclear.

戒不可不持，戒不持則人天路絕；行不可不修，行不修則功德不圓；經不可不讀，經不讀則理路不明；

Practice meditation,
Or your mind will be impure.
Understand the teachings,
Or you will encounter obstacles.

禪不可不參，禪不參則心地不透；道不可不悟，道不悟則觸目成滯。

A word of Truth is priceless;
It is a thousand times more precious
Than gold or silver.
Human virtue is priceless;
It is a thousand times higher
Than the highest mountain.

一句真理無價寶，比金比銀萬倍好；人間道德無價寶，比山比嶽萬倍高。

A tolerant mind can embrace "big" and "more".
A responsible courage can bear honor and shame.
A decisive wisdom can determine right and wrong.

包容的心胸，要包容大與多；承擔的勇氣，要承擔榮與辱；決斷的智慧，要決斷是與非。

A kind-hearted moment
Will bring endless merit.
A pure-hearted moment
Will bring innumerable virtue.
An enlightened moment
Will bring infinite wonder.
A pure, empty-minded moment
Will bring the origin of no-notion.

剎那的善心可得無盡的福報，剎那的淨心可得無量的功德，剎那的悟心可得無限的妙覺，剎那的空心可得無相的本體。

One useful word is worth more
Than innumerable, useless words;
One beneficial event is better
Than all sorts of useless hardships.

有用的話一句，勝於無益的千言萬語；有益的事一件，勝於無用的千辛萬苦。

One kind word is like the fragrance of flowers
In paradise.
One harsh word is like a sword
In hell.

一句善心美言，即是天堂的花香；一聲瞋恨惡語，即成地獄的刀劍。

Happiness is the bait
That poisons determinations;
Suffering is the foundry
That forms saints and sages.

安樂是鴆殺志氣的毒餌，患難是陶鑄聖賢的洪爐。

A quick learner
Is not necessarily smart.
A slow learner
Is not necessarily stupid.

舉一知十，未必是聰明之輩；舉十知一，未必是愚蠢之人。

Being unconventional
Does not necessarily mean outstanding.
Being mild
Does not necessarily mean unkeen.

詭言標異，未必有卓越之處；言行平淡，未必非睿智之人。

Like a pyramid -
Learning
Should be wide and tall.
Like saints and sages -
To get along with people
One should have merit, wisdom and character.

為學要如金字塔，要能廣博要能高；為人要如聖賢德，要有福慧有根基。

A little sincerity -
All conditions respond.
A lot of gratefulness -
The world is joyful.

一念誠心，諸緣感應；十分懷恩，人天歡喜。

To urge others to be good,
You must first be upright yourself; i.e.,
"Do what I do." is better than "Do what I say."
To dispute rumors,
You must first be upstanding; i.e.,
"Facts speak louder than words."

要勸化別人，首演端正自己，此乃「身教勝於言教」；要辯解譏毀，先要健全自己，所謂「事實勝於雄辯」。

Aspiring to the right teachings,
One must first have the right mind.
Entering into the right teachings,
One must be able to let go.
Practicing the right teachings,
One must use compassionate wisdom.
Manifesting the right teachings,
One must comprehend no-self.

欲求正道，須先正心；欲入正道，須能放下；欲行正道，須運悲智；欲證正道，須悟無我。

Where the Dharma exists, the Buddha exists;
Believing in the Dharma is believing in the Buddha.
Where the Sangha resides, the Dharma resides;
Believing in the Sangha is believing in the Dharma.

　　法在則佛在，信法就是信佛；僧住則法住，信僧就是信法。

Without cultivation,
You cannot liberate yourself.
Without preaching the Dharma,
You cannot liberate all beings.

不修行，無以度自己；不說法，無以度眾生。

Attribute glory to the Buddha;
Attribute accomplishments to all beings;
Attribute benefits to the monastics;
Attribute merits to devotees.

光榮歸於佛陀，成就歸於大眾，利益歸於常住，功德歸於信徒。

Fame and wealth are transitory;
Only achievement and character are genuine joy.
The world is like a house on fire;
Only calming body and mind is true pure land.

功名富貴轉眼空，唯立功、立德才是真受用；世間三界皆火宅，唯安身、安心才是好淨土。

Understanding classical lessons
Can warn the mind.
Limiting alcohol and sex
Can purify the mind.
Eliminating personal desire can cultivate the mind.
Perceiving the truth
Can clear the mind.

明古訓可以儆心，寡酒色可以清心，袪私欲可以養心，悟至理可以明心。

The breeze feels cool and lovely;
Kind words feel gentle and loving.

微風吹人只覺清爽可愛，愛語告人何等溫柔可親。

People who are rich in heart -
For the favor of one drop of water,
They will return a fountain.
People who are poor in heart -
To give one thing away
Is as difficult for them as climbing to the sky.

心地富有者，滴水之恩湧泉以報；心地貧窮者，一物之施難如登天。

Before learning,
One should focus
On pursuing what one wants to learn.
After learning,
One should focus
On applying what one has already learned.

未知時，宜一心一意求其所欲知；既知後，當一心一意行其所已知。

Language should be fluent,
But more importantly be proper.
Clothes should be simple,
But more importantly be suitable.

語言重流利，更重得體；衣著重樸素，更重合宜。

Essays should be idiomatic,
But more importantly be significant.
Expression should be precise,
But more importantly be sincere.

文章重通暢，更重內涵；表達重明確，更重真誠。

Making earnest efforts to cultivate virtue
Is the shortcut to getting along with people.
Forming affinities
Is the resource for handling affairs.

精進是做人的捷徑，結緣是辦事的資糧。

Better to observe the precepts imperfectly
Than to misunderstand the teachings,
And thereby lose faith in them.

寧可持戒不圓滿，不可破見失道心。

Using useless words
To occupy useful time
Not only makes people disgusted
But also virtueless.

以無益的話語去佔有用的時間，不僅使人討厭，簡直是無德之行；

Using useful time
To do useless things
Not only is unhelpful
But also a waste of life.

以有用的時間去做無用的事情，不但無補時益，簡直是糟蹋人生。

Don't rush, don't rush, safety first.
Don't rush, don't rush, modesty first.
Don't rush, don't rush, courtesy first.

不急，不急，安全第一！不急，不急，謙讓第一！不急，不急，禮貌第一！

Indulgence
Is the root of all evil.
Diligence
Is the key to good deeds.

放逸是眾惡之本，勤勇是善行之要。

Use some thought to counter evil thought;
Use right thought to counter absurd thought;
Use no-thought to counter right thought..

以有念對治邪念，以正念對治妄念，以無念對治正念。

Don't try to use just a little knowledge
To acquire a lot of honor;
Use all of your ability
To bear most of the duty;

勿以少分的學德，博取多分的榮譽；應以十分的才幹，擔負八分的任務；

Use full preparation
To teach a complete course;
Use all your heart
To return even a small favor.

97　要用萬分的準備，教授全分的課程；雖受一分的恩惠，也報百分的心意。

Accomplishing the teachings
Depends on self;
Applying the teachings
Depends on time;
Perfecting the teachings
Depends on people;
Proving the teachings
Depends on cultivation.

道之成在我，道之行在時，道之美在人，道之證在修。

Scorn - bear it.
Adversity - endure it.
Then, difficulty will bow to you.

受得起別人的冷落，禁得起外境的磨難，困難就會向你低頭。

Use encouragement
To replace criticism;
Use kindness
To replace scolding;
Use caring
To replace dissipation;
Use cooperation
To replace aloofness.

以鼓勵代替責備，以慈愛代替呵罵，以關懷代替放縱，以同事代替隔閡。

Other Books Available in English
by Venerable Master Hsing Yun

The Hundred Sayings Series
Happily Ever After
Perfectly Willing
The Philosophy of Being Second (forthcoming)

The Humanistic Buddhism Series
How I Practice Humanistic Buddhism
Where Is Your Buddha Nature?

The Lion's Roar
Hsing Yun's Ch'an Talks
Epoch of the Buddha's Light
Carefree Life

Being Good: Buddhist Ethics for Everyday Life
Only a Great Rain: A Guide to Chinese Buddhist Meditation
These newest publications are also available through major booksellers.

English Monthly Booklets Available

These previously released publications from the Fo Guang Shan International Translation Center are available as follows:

- *The Essence of Ch'an*
- *The Diamond Sutra and the Study of Wisdom and Emptiness*
- *The Wheel of Rebirth*
- *A Discussion on Perception and Understanding*
- *The Amitabha Sutra and the Pure Land School*
- *The Fundamental Concepts of Humanistic Buddhism*
- *On Becoming A Bodhisattva*

- *Speaking of Love and Affection*
- *Worldly Living, Transcendental Practice*
- *A Glimpse of Ch'an through the Sixth Patriarch's Platform Sutra*
- *When We Die*
- *Seeing the Buddha*